I hope yo

Women of the Old Testament

By

Leslie A. Johnson

Copyright © 2023 Leslie A. Johnson All rights reserved

No part of this book may be reproduced, or stored in a retrieval system, or transmitted in any form or by any means, electronic, mechanical, photocopying, recording, or otherwise, without express written permission of the author or publisher.

Cover design by: Leslie Johnson

Printed in the United States of America

Introduction

Women of the Old Testament demonstrates how women, in the lower social class era, provided strength and courage in each of the women selected.

When God called, the women in the Old Testament, not just answered, but fought the good fight.

Table of Contents

Introduction 5

Eve 9

Sarah 12

Lot's Wife 17

Rahab 21

Hannah 25

Rebekah 32

Miriam 41

Ruth 44

Abigail 47

Deborah 50

Huldah 53

Esther 57

Meet the Author 61

Books by Same Author 62

Saved 70

Bible 73

Dedicated to 75

Eve

Eve would the most heard of and the most popular woman known in the Bible. Adam, the man, and Eve, the woman, were the first human creations of God. God created Adam and then Eve because God did not want Adam to be alone. "The man called his wife Eve because she was the mother of all living" (Genesis 3:20 ESV).

Adam and Eve were supposed to rule over everything in the Garden of Eden. God told them: They could eat from any fruit from the trees except for the "Tree of knowledge of Good and Evil". God warned them that if they ate from the tree, they would die.

The serpent, devil or Satan, deceived Eve by twisting God's words around so she ate from the tree.

"When the woman saw that the fruit of the tree was good for food and pleasing to the eye, and desirable for gaining wisdom, she took some and ate it. She also gave some to Adam, who was with her, and he ate some.

Then the eyes of both of them were opened, and they realized they were naked; so, they sewed fig leaves together and made coverings for themselves" (Genesis 3:6-7).

God was not happy as He told them they could eat from everything except from the "Tree of Knowledge of Good and Evil". God gave Eve three punishments. "To the woman He said, "I will make your pains in childbearing very severe; with painful labor you will give birth to children. Your desire will be for your husband, and he will rule over you" (Gen. 3:16). Both Adam and Eve were kicked out of the Garden of Eden.

Eve bore three sons named in the Bible: Cain, Abel, and Seth and "other sons and daughters." Eve is the first woman, wife, and mother in history. Also, the first mother of a murderer in history.

Explanation:

All of this because Eve did not obey God as she was tempted by Satan. We are tempted every day, but I am pretty sure we do not see the devil as we are tempted as Eve was tempted by the serpent. We all face trials and tribulations in life, some less and some more, but we face them head on and hopefully we stay on course and our faith does not whither.

Sarah

Sarah, originally named Saria, was the first wife of Abraham. Sarah was the only woman in the Bible whose name was changed by God. Sarah wanted children. She was childless until she was 80 years old.

God promised Abraham that she would be "a mother of nations" (Genesis 17:16) and that she would conceive and bear a son, but Sarah did not believe.

Sarah did not believe she sent her handmaid, Hagar, to Abraham so they would be able to have children. Hagar did have a son, Ishmael.

This was not how God intended for Abraham and Sarah. Once Ishmael was born, both Sarah and Hagar fought over jealousy and bitter words.

God told Abraham: "'I will certainly return to you according to the time of life, and behold, Sarah your wife shall have a son.' (Sarah was listening in the tent door which was behind him)" (Genesis 18:10). At first Sarah laughed and was little of faith. In verses 12-13: "Therefore Sarah laughed within herself, saying, 'After I have grown old, shall I have pleasure, my lord being old also?' And the

LORD said to Abraham, 'Why did Sarah laugh, saying, 'Shall I surely bear a child, since I am old?'" Then she asked, "Is there anything too hard for the Lord?"

"Now Sarah was listening at the entrance to the tent, which was behind him. Abraham and Sarah were already very old, and Sarah was past the age of childbearing. So, Sarah laughed to herself as she thought, "After I am worn out and my lord is old, will I now have this pleasure?

Then the Lord said to Abraham, "Why did Sarah laugh and say, 'Will I really have a child, now that I am old?' Is anything too hard for the Lord? I will return to you at the appointed time next year, and Sarah will have a son."

"Sarah was afraid, so she lied and said, "I did not laugh."

But he said, "Yes, you did laugh" (Gen. 18:10-15).

"Now the Lord was gracious to Sarah as he had said, and the Lord did for Sarah what he had promised. Sarah became pregnant and bore a son to Abraham in his old age, at the very time God had promised him.

Abraham gave the name Isaac to the son Sarah bore him. When his son Isaac was eight days old, Abraham circumcised him, as God commanded him. Abraham was a hundred years old when his son Isaac was born to him.

Sarah said, "God has brought me laughter, and everyone who hears about this will laugh with me." And she added, "Who would have said to Abraham that Sarah would nurse children? Yet I have borne him a son in his old age" (Gen. 21:1-7).

Explanation:

Sarah had her doubts and made them known to God with her laughing. Sarah gave her husband another woman to take her place to sleep with Abraham, and to become pregnant. While this might have been the practice back then, why could not Sarah wait on God.

God already told Abraham he would make him father of all nations and told Sarah she would bare a child.

Waiting on God's timing, not ours. God is outside of time, so we must wait patiently on His timing.

When God says He will do something or tell you this or that will happen, be patient God's perfect will.

God wants the best for everyone, and He takes no pleasure in punishing or scolding someone. There is nothing too big for God. Lay your troubles and sorrows, even your blessings at God's feet, and He will Hear you.

Lot's Wife

Lot, the nephew of Abraham, had a wife and no name were mentioned in the Bible. One day, Lot was sitting by the gate of Sodom and two messengers came to him. Lot invited them to stay overnight.

Lot's wife, we could assume she cooked it, prepared a meal for everyone. Then a crowd gathered outside of Lot's house, and they wanted him to bring out the two messengers, but Lot offered his two virgin daughters instead of the messengers, but they still wanted the messengers,

A bright light came into the crowd as they tried to go through the door of Lot's house and the bright light blinded them so they could not see the entrance.

The messengers told Lot to flee with his family as Sodom is about to be destroyed. "As dawn broke, the messengers urged Lot on, saying, "Up, take your wife and your two remaining daughters, lest you be swept away because of the iniquity of the city" (Gen, 19:15, The Contemporary Torah, JPS, 2006).

Lot and his family did not leave yet, so the two messengers took his hand and brought them outside the gate of Sodom.

"When they had brought them outside, one said, "Flee for your life! Do not look behind you, nor stop anywhere in the Plain; flee to the hills, lest you be swept away" (19:17).

They were told not to look back. "Lot's wife looked back, and she thereupon turned into a pillar of salt" (19:26). Lot's wife, nameless turned into a pillar of salt. Jesus referenced her in Luke 17:32 saying, "Remember Lot's wife!" Jesus was talking about the last days.

Explanation:

Trust in God's plan. Do not turn against God's commands. Have faith in God. He knows all! The Lord will always lead. Lot's wife could have been a non-believer and that is why she turned back. Take faith and believe what God has said through His Word and prayer.

In the teaching in Zephaniah 1:12, "I will search Jerusalem with lamps, and I will punish the men who are complacent, those who say in their hearts, 'the Lord will not do good, nor will he do ill.'" The man who believes, yet physically allows the flesh to be satisfied by the world, denies God's righteousness. Do not worry about earthly possessions as we are Christians and keep our eye on God.

Rahab

Rahab is known for being a harlot or a prostitute. Although, she played a big role in society in the Old Testament days.

Joshua sent spies into the city of Jericho to check out the city Israel was to conquer. Rahab, a woman of ill reputation, took in the spies and when the King's men asked her to turn them over, she hid Joshua's men in her attic. Then, she lied to the king's men, telling them the spies "went that away!" Off the king's men went, never finding the spies.

A short time later, the army of Israel marched around Jericho for six days. On the seventh, they blew the trumpets and the walls fell.

Rahab's faith, a belief that the spies were men of God, saved her and her family. This led to a series of remarkable events.

Rahab made choices in her life. She chose to believe God's choice. Rahab decision to hide the spies led to the conquering of Jericho. A woman at the bottom of the social ladder made her decision which led her to marry Salmon who had a son, Boaz. Boaz married Ruth (remember this for later).

Rahab chose to take a leap of faith. "By faith the prostitute Rahab, because she welcomed the spies, was not killed with those who were disobedient" (Hebrews 11:31, NIV).

Explanation:

Choices were available to Rahab. One bad choice could have meant between life and death and destruction. She took the leap of faith and made wise decisions. Who would believe a harlot? Well, the people searching did and this one choice saved her life.

Rahab would go on to make other choices. She believed the men were sent from God. Hebrews 11 is known as the Faith Chapter, and it opens with a description of faith: "Faith is the substance of things hoped for, the evidence of things not seen" (Hebrews 11:1).

It goes on to show that it is impossible to please God without faith (verse 6). Rahab had that faith.

Harlotry considered was not shameful in the Canaanite culture. Her house was divided into an inn. Travelers would come and go. Rahab risked it all and put her trust in God.

Rahab had faith and acted upon it. It was not just good works but faith. We all can learn that faith needs good works.

This is a great lesson we can learn: like Rahab, we must act on our faith. It is not enough to just have faith and believe in God, we must act on it through obedience. As James also wrote, "Faith without works is dead" (James 2:26).

We must read about all the miracles in the Bible, just like Rahab read or heard it through the pipeline or by word of mouth. As Christians we believe in the miracles because we put out faith in God.

Hannah

Hannah was in deep anguish at not having a child. She prayed at the temple day and night to have a child. Hannah never gave up hope that God would hear her prayer. Hannah knew the right words in prayer, and she knew when to keep quiet.

In the biblical narrative, Hannah is one of two wives of Elkanah. The other, Peninnah, had given birth to Elkanah's children, but Hannah remained childless.

"When the day came that Elkanah sacrificed, he would give portions to his wife Peninnah and to all her sons and daughters; but to Hannah he would give a double portion, because he loved Hannah, but the Lord had closed her womb. Her rival, moreover, would provoke her bitterly to irritate her, because the Lord had closed her womb. And it happened year after year, as often as she went up to the house of the Lord, that she would provoke her; so, she wept and would not eat. Then Elkanah her husband would say to her, "Hannah, why do you weep, and why do you not eat, and why is your heart sad? Am I not better to you than ten sons?"

"Then Hannah got up after eating and drinking in Shiloh. Now Eli the priest was sitting on the seat by the doorpost of the temple of the Lord. She, distressed, prayed to the Lord and wept bitterly. And she made a vow and said, "Lord of armies, if You will indeed look on the affliction of Your bondservant and remember me, and not forget Your bondservant, but will give Your bondservant a son, then I will give him to the Lord all the days of his life, and a razor shall never come on his head" (1 Samuel 1:4-11, NASB).

Hannah cried and would not eat as she wanted a child. She wanted a son, which the son would carry on with his father, but as we have seen in the *Women in the Bible*, women can carry on by their selves. Hannah went back on to the temple, praying to the Lord, and Eli watched her mouth. "As for Hannah, she was speaking in her heart, only her lips were quivering, but her voice was not heard. So, Eli thought that she was drunk. Then Eli said to her, "How long will you behave like a drunk? Get rid of your wine!" But Hannah answered and said, "No, my lord, I am a woman despairing in spirit; I have drunk neither wine nor strong drink, but I have poured out my soul before the Lord. Do not consider your bondservant a useless woman, for I have spoken until now out of my great concern and provocation." Then Eli answered and said, "Go in peace; and may the God of Israel grant your request that you have asked of Him." She said, "Let your bondservant find favor in your sight." So, the woman went on her way and ate, and her face was no longer sad. "(1 Samuel 1:13-18, NASB).

"Then they got up early in the morning and worshiped before the Lord and returned to their house in Ramah. And Elkanah had relations with Hannah his wife, and the Lord remembered her. It came about in due time, after Hannah had conceived, that she gave birth to a son; and she named him Samuel, saying, "Because I have asked for him of the Lord."

Hannah, after weaning Samuel, brought him to the temple where her prayers and tears poured out asking of the Lord to give her a son. She did what she promised and dedicated Samuel to the Lord. Samuel went on to be a major prophet involved in the likes of David.

Explanation:

Hannah never gave up hope of having a child. She was a victim of verbal abuse, all because she had no child. Hannah in the Bible is found only in 1 Samuel, yet her story is anything but insignificant. Hannah's story deals with infertility, bullying, answered prayer and reaches prophetically into the New Testament.

She took her pain to the only one could alleviate it, which was God. She encountered with negatively from the other wife to Eli the priest in the temple who accuses her as being drunk. She was not drunk but tears fell like rain.

Giving birth to Samuel was only part of the big picture. She dedicated him to the Lord her

God. After Samuel, she had five more children.

After Hannah fulfilled her vow delivering Samuel to the temple, she worshipped and sang prophetically. In 1 Samuel 2:1-10, is "The Song of Hannah: "Then Hannah prayed and said: "My heart rejoices in the Lord; in the Lord my horn is lifted high. My mouth boasts over my enemies, for I delight in your deliverance. "There is no one holy like the Lord; there is no one besides you; there is no Rock like our God. "Do not keep talking so proudly or let your mouth speak such arrogance, for the Lord is a God who knows, and by him deeds are weighed. "The bows of the warriors are broken, but those who stumbled are armed with strength. Those who were full hire themselves out for food, but those who were hungry are hungry no more. She who was barren has borne seven children, but she who has had many sons' pines away. "The Lord brings death and makes alive; he brings down to the grave and raises up. The Lord sends poverty and wealth; he humbles, and he exalts. He raises the poor from the dust and lifts the needy from the ash heap; he seats them with princes and has them inherit a throne of honor. "For the foundations of the earth are the Lord's; on them he has set the world. He will guard the feet of his faithful servants, but the wicked will be silenced in the place of darkness. "It is not by strength that one prevails; those who oppose the Lord will be broken. The Highest will thunder from heaven; the Lord will judge the ends of the earth. "He will give strength to his king and exalt the horn of his anointed" (NIV).

Amen!!

Rebekah

Rebekah is the daughter-in-law of Abraham and Sarah. She married Isaac. The story of Rebekah is in Genesis 24, which is the longest chapter in the Book of Genesis.

A servant swore an oath to Abraham to set out in his homeland to find a wife for Isaac. The Lord blessed the servant. The servant found a well and said, ""O Lord, God of my master Abraham, please grant me success today and show steadfast love to my master Abraham. Behold, I am standing by the spring of water, and the daughters of the men of the city are coming out to draw water. Let the young woman to whom I shall say, 'Please let down your jar that I may drink,' and who shall say, 'Drink, and I will water your camels'—let her be the one whom you have appointed for your servant Isaac. By this I shall know that you have shown steadfast love to my master." And "Before he had finished speaking, behold, Rebekah, who was born to Bethuel the son of Milcah, the wife of Nahor, Abraham's brother, came out with her water jar on her shoulder. The young woman was very attractive in appearance, a maiden who not had known. She went down to the spring and filled her jar and came up. Then the servant ran to meet her and said, "Please give me a little water to drink from your jar." She said, "Drink, my lord." And she quickly let down her jar upon her hand and gave him a drink. When she had finished giving him a drink, she said, "I will draw water for your camels also, until they have finished drinking." So, she quickly emptied her jar into the trough and ran again to the well to draw water, and she drew for all his camels. The man gazed at her in silence to learn whether the Lord had prospered his journey or not" (Ch. 24:7-21, ESV).

The servant and Rebekah went to her home so the servant could ask her father. The father asked Rebekah if that is what she wanted and she said yes. "But he said to me, 'The Lord, before whom I have walked, will send his angel with you and prosper your way. You shall take a wife for my son from my clan and from my father's house" (24: 40).

After Rebeca said yes, the men blessed her. "And they blessed Rebekah and said to her,

"Our sister, may you become

    thousands of ten thousands,

and may your offspring possess

    the gate of those who hate him!"

Then Rebekah and her young women arose and rode on the camels and followed the man. Thus, the servant took Rebekah and went his way" (Ch. 24:60-61). Rebekah went with the servant back to Abraham.

Rebekah was baren so Isaak prayed to the Lord, and the Lord answered his prayer and Rebekah became pregnant, not just one, but the Lord doubled, and she was pregnant with twins.

"The children struggled together within her, and she said, "If it is thus, why is this happening to me?" So, she went to inquire of the Lord. And the Lord said to her,

"Two nations are in your womb, and two peoples from within you shall be divided; the one shall be stronger than the other, the older shall serve the younger" (24:22-23).

The first baby to come out had red hair and they called him, Esau. The second baby came out holding Esau's heel, so they named him Jacob.

There was famine in the land, so Isaak set out for Gerar. "And the Lord appeared to him and said, "Do not go down to Egypt; dwell in the land of which I shall tell you. Sojourn in this land, and I will be with you and will bless you, for to you and to your offspring I will give all these lands, and I will establish the oath that I swore to Abraham your father. I will multiply your offspring as the stars of heaven and will give to your offspring all these lands. And in your offspring, all the nations of the earth shall be blessed, because Abraham obeyed my voice and kept my charge, my commandments, my statutes, and my laws. So, Isaac settled in Gerar. When the men of the place asked him about his wife, he said, "She is my sister," for he feared to say, "My wife," thinking, "lest the men of the place should kill me because of Rebekah," because she was attractive in appearance. (26:2-7). We can find this earlier with Abraham calling his wife, Sarah, his sister. So, this is a theme going on with Sarah and Rebekah.

Isaac, now an old man with eyes that could barely see, called in Esau the eldest son. Isaac told Esau to go hunt for him to make food for him so he could bless Esau before he dies. Rebekah was listening by the door and told Jacob to do the same as he was her favorite.

"But Jacob said to Rebekah his mother, "Behold, my brother Esau is a hairy man, and I am a smooth man. Perhaps my father will feel me, and I shall seem to be mocking him and bring a curse upon myself and not a blessing." His mother said to him, "Let your curse be on me, my son; only obey my voice, and go, bring them to me" (Genesis 26:11-13). Rebekah wanted Jacob to be blessed as the first child is blessed and the line of succession stays with the first-born son.

"Then his father Isaac said to him, "Come near and kiss me, my son." So, he came near and kissed him. And Isaac smelled the smell of his garments and blessed him and said, "See, the smell of my son is as the smell of a field that the Lord has blessed! May God give you of the dew of heaven and of the fatness of the earth and plenty of grain and wine. Let people serve you and nations bow down to you. Be lord over your brothers and may your mother's sons bow down to you. Cursed be everyone who curses you, and blessed be everyone who blesses you!" (26:26-29). Rebekah and Jacob tricked and took advantage of Isaac's blindness and blessed the wrong child.

Explanation:

God blessed the servant and Isaac but also blessed Rebekah. Rebekah gives birth to twin sons. After years of barrenness and gains the primary place in the lineage for her younger son, Jacob. He is destined to become the ancestor of all Israel. The trickery and manipulation of Rebekah could mean she is assertive and worthy woman. Although this type of manipulation should not happen in today's world, unless Lord God wants it to be.

To note that in Genesis 24:67, Isaac declares his love for her. It is the first time a woman in the Hebrew Bible whom matrimonial love is communicated.

Scholars estimate Isaak's age of the manipulation was between 132 and 137. For some reason, people lived longer in the Old Testament. I will let you produce your own conclusions and ponder over it to know why.

The nation of Israel came from Jacob, and the line of Esau became the Edomites.

Miriam

Miriam was a known in the bible as the sister to Aaron and Moses. She helped Moses to lead the people of Israel out of Slavery in Egypt. "Then Miriam with prophetess, the sister of Aaron, took a tambourine in her hand, and you all the women went out after her with tambourines and dancing. And Miriam sang to them: "Sing to the Lord, for he has triumphed gloriously; the horse and his rider he has thrown into the sea" (Exodus 15:20-21).

"Miriam and Aaron spoke against Moses because of the Cushite woman whom he had married, for he had married a Cushite woman" (Numbers 12:1).

"And suddenly the Lord said to Moses and to Aaron and Miriam, "Come out, you three, to the tent of meeting." And the three of them came out.

And the Lord came down in a pillar of cloud and stood at the entrance of the tent and called Aaron and Miriam, and they both came forward.

When the cloud removed from over the tent, behold, Miriam was leprous, like snow. And Aaron turned toward Miriam, and behold, she was leprous. So, Miriam was shut outside the camp seven days, and the people did not set out on the march till Miriam was brought in again" (Numbers 12:4-5, 10-15).

Miriam and Aaron both criticized Moses, God's chosen servant, wife constantly. This made God angry because how both spoke to His chosen one.

Explanation:

Remember how we treat people; you never know the time of Jesus' coming. Also, you do not know if God chose a person. Miriam started out leading the way for the women, but at the end she turned ill for verbal abuse of one woman.

Ruth

Ruth has her own book in the Hebrew Bible called Ruth. The Book of Ruth has a famous saying in it, but most people do not know it came from a woman, Ruth says, ""Do not urge me to leave you or to return from following you. For where you go, I will go, and where you lodge, I will lodge. Your people shall be my people, and your God my God.

Where you die, I will die, and there I will be buried. May the LORD do so to me and more also if anything but death parts me from you" (Ruth 16-18).

Ruth was "the woman of Moab. She as related to Israel through Lot. Ruth lived in the period of Judges. Ruth's husband and only brother passed away so the decision for her to make was to stay in her home in Moab or go with her mother-in-law Naomi to Judah.

They both stopped their traveling in Bethlehem and Ruth's faith and testimony spread through Judah. Boaz heard great things about Ruth and said,

"All that you have done for your mother-in-law since the death of your husband has been fully told to me, and how you left your father and mother and your native land and came to a people that you did not know before. The LORD repay you for what you have done, and a full reward be given you by the LORD, the God of Israel, under whose wings you have come to take refuge!" (Ruth 2:11-12).

Redemption appears in the Book of Ruth over twenty-three times. I sense a theme here. Boaz redeems and marries Ruth and bought back Naomi's Land. Ruth was a Gentile, meaning not Jewish.

Explanation:

A faithful friend who helps each other out in need. The word redemption was used over twenty-three times in the Book of Ruth. Ho can we bring about redemption in our lives? Redemption can mean salvation, restoration, or recovery.

Abigail

A courageous woman in 1 Samuel 25, named

Abigail. She as married to a wealthy man, but

he did not know social graces or how closely he was to be killed if it was not for his wife, Abigail.

Abigail combined wisdom and her best social graces to turn away a fierce army. An army led by David! David and four hundred men were on their way. One of Abigail's servants told her about the approaching David and his army.

Abigail used her wisdom and wit to load up her donkeys and went out to meet David.

When Abigail saw David, without any word fell at his feet. She gave a warm and heartfelt for David to spare her husband and household. She humbled herself in front of David.

She even admitted her husband was a bad person. Abigail reminded David of his enemies and about his past on the run from King Saul.

Abigail humble request turned David's heart. David saw the erroneousness he was about to make. David sent her away with the promise to her safe passage and her household.

In the face of danger, Abigail faced danger in the face and with humility and humility.

Explanation:

David was about to kill a man just because of an insult. Even though he was of bad character, we all could learn from the husband, Abigail, and David. Abigail humbled herself in front of a mighty king and warrior.

David reminded of his ways and learned from his past.

Deborah

The story of Deborah in Judges 4 and 5 begins like many of the stories in the Book of Judges—the Israelites sinned against the Lord, and he sold them out to King Jabin of Canaan. This went on for 20 years until the Israelites cried out to the Lord for help. At that time, Deborah was leading Israel as a judge. She sent for Barak, a commander in Israel's army, and told him to go and fight Jabin's army led by Sisera.

Barak said he would only go if Deborah went with him. Deborah agreed but told Barak the honor will not go to him, because the Lord will deliver Sisera into the hands of a woman. When Barak's army advances, the Lord routs Sisera's army, and Sisera flees on foot. Sisera goes to the tent of Jael, the wife of Heber, because there was an alliance between King Jabin and Heber's family.

Jael invited Sisera in and served him refreshments. Sisera was so exhausted, he fell asleep. Jael took a hammer and pounded a tent peg into Sisera's temple, killing him. The Israelites fought against King Jabin until they destroyed him. Deborah and Barak sang a song of praise, and Israel had peace for 40 years. (Otten, n.d).

Deborah answered the call by God and defeated the army. She states, "The villagers ceased in Israel; they ceased to be until I arose; I, Deborah, arose as a mother in Israel. When new gods were chosen, then war was in the gates. Was shield or spear to be seen among forty thousand in Israel? My heart goes out to the commanders of Israel who offered themselves willingly among the people. Bless the Lord" (Judges 5:7-9).

Explanation:

Deborah was a Judge, or a warrior hen Israel cried out that they anted ones. The Israelites were in slavery for about 20 years. They needed someone or anyone to inspire them. This inspiration coming from a woman in this era just shows how God does not show partiality or prejudice. When calls be willing to answer that call.

Deborah was the only one called a prophet. The Lord calls ordinary people to do extraordinary things. Anything accomplished with the Holy Spirit.

Huldah

Also called Huldah the Prophetess. A woman to deliver a message chosen by God. God sent prophets to send His people back to them or to deliver a message and warnings. Israel and Judah went back to their sinful ways.

After David and Solomon, the kingdom split in two and the people began to wander from God into wickedness and disobedience. There were occasional good and faithful kings, but most were not. Repeatedly, God sent prophets to call them to return to the Lord, to return to their first love. Elijah and Elisha, Micah and Amos, Ezekiel and Jeremiah were all sent by the Lord to speak his word so the people would repent and return. Sometimes the people listened, and sometimes they did not. One of the lesser-known prophets, though no less significant, was a woman named Huldah (Otten, n.d.).

At the mere age of eight, Josiah became king of Judah. He did what was right in the eyes of the Lord. The Bible tells us that he was the first, and only, king who loved God with all his heart, soul, and might (2 Kings 23:25). Josiah was sincere and upright.

A key turning point in Josiah's reign occurred in his 18th year as king. While cleansing the Temple, Hilkiah, the high priest, discovered the Book of the Law (a form of Deuteronomy). When the book was read to him, Josiah tore his robes in grief. He and God's people had not obeyed the words of this book. They had fallen short and had not done those things which they ought to have done. They had fallen short of what God commanded them to do. Josiah knew that God must have been angry with them.

Seeking reconciliation with God, Josiah sent Hilkiah the priest and four other men to speak to the prophetess Huldah. Huldah, married to Shallum, keeper of the king's robes, was a scholar of high rank in Jerusalem. She was a woman of authority, and people listened to what she said. These men were no exception.

Huldah prophesied to them, saying God was about to bring disaster to this place and these people, according to all that Josiah had read. Because they had abandoned God and sought other lovers—idols—God's anger would burn against the people for what they had done. They could not escape destruction and would be punished for abandoning God. However, because Josiah had repented and humbled himself before God, tore his robes and wept in God's presence, Josiah would die in peace. He would be spared. He had done his best to lead his people back to God, and so God would let him die before destruction would be brought upon them (Otten, n. d).

Her prophecies always came true. A prophet is someone God is spoken to or is speaking through them to give warnings and messages.

Explanations:

The Holy Spirit was working through Huldah. Not many men, let alone a woman to advise anyone, especially a king back in that era as enormous.

She only mentioned in the Hebrew Bible in 2 Kings 22:14-20 and 2 Chronicles 34:22-28. Although, Huldah voice and leadership inspires men and women.

Esther

Esther was a young Jewish woman. She is described as beautiful and obedient. Esther has her Book in the Bible called Esther. She finds favor with king Ahasuerus. She had to hide her Jewish faith.

Esther one theme is feasting. "and in the third year of his reign he gave a banquet for all his nobles and officials. The military leaders of Persia and Media, the princes, and the nobles of the provinces were present" (Esther, 1:3).

And in fasting:

"Go, gather together all the Jews who are in Susa, and fast for me. Do not eat or drink for three days, night or day. I and my attendants will fast as you do. When this is done, I will go to the king, even though it is against the law. And if I perish, I perish" (Esther, 4:16, NIV).

"Esther proved to have a godly and teachable spirit that also showed great strength and willing obedience. Esther's humility was markedly different from the attitude of those around her, and this caused her to be elevated into the position of queen. She shows us that remaining respectful and humble, even in difficult if not humanly impossible circumstances, often sets us up to be the vessel of untold blessing for both us and others. We would do well to emulate her godly attitudes in all areas of life, but especially in trials. Not once is there a complaint or bad attitude exposed in the writing. Many times, we read she won the "favor" of those around her. Such a favor is what saved her people. We can be granted such favor as we accept even unfair persecution and follow Esther's example of maintaining a positive attitude, coupled with humility and the determination to lean on God. Who knows but that God put us in such a position, for just such a time as this" (Got Questions, n.d.).

Esther marries King Ahasuerus. Her uncle Mordecai raised her because she was an orphan. Mordecai tells Esther about a plot to kill the king. Esther tells her husband and king about the plot.

Explanation:

Esther, an orphan, married a king. God has a hand in this, but the word God is not in the Book of Esther. Although the Book of Esther is to show the providence to God and His chosen people.

Esther showed to display her act of courage as she told the king about the plot to kill him.

Meet the Author

Kiya and I.

Books by Same Author

Anxiety, Depression, and the Bible

Being in a wheelchair is difficult, add Anxiety and Depression to it, then it is a recipe for disaster. What does it say in the Bible about Anxiety and Depression? Finding out was Leslie Johnson's goal as he suffers from the conditions. How can Leslie's go beyond his depression of getting older? Well, what has God said to Leslie? These questions must be asked for him to find answers to guide and comfort Leslie in his time of sorrow and weakness. Leslie must look at what God has said to him or his fellow brothers and sisters in Christ and in Scripture. Leslie knows the Bible says faith comes from hearing the Word of Christ. Depression can be difficult but not by not hearing the Word of God. Leslie needed to hear the Word of God. It is time he heard and read the Holy Scriptures

Thirty Wise Sayings of the Bible

In the book of Proverbs, is a hidden treasure called: The Thirty Sayings of the Wise. Please join Leslie Johnson on the quest of the wise.

Wisdom in Psalm

Wisdom in Psalms reflects on wisdom, on the fate of the righteous and the wicked, and on the Law. They are distinguished by their reflective, meditative tone, and their didactic character.

Wise Sayings in Ecclesiastes

The Wise Sayings in Ecclesiastes is a collection of sayings from Solomon, David, and God.

Finding wisdom in the different books of the Bible. Wisdom in the books of Proverbs, Ecclesiastes, and in Psalms.

The Book of Job Summary

The Book of Job is about death, suffering, free will, and God's mercy and grace. I am not positive who authored the book of Job.

I do my best, in my interpretation to give you the summary of Job. Without any philosophical debates, I try my best to give you the substance.

Dad on Wheels

Dad on Wheels is a wonderful story about a father and son learning to navigate life with the challenges of a disability. A father in a wheelchair, and a son with questions, this sweet book offers some insight for children that may show curiosity about a wheelchair bound friend or loved one. Read and enjoy.

Saved

If you want to know Jesus Christ as your Savior, then you just pray the following prayer: Dear Lord Jesus, I know that I am a sinner, and I ask for Your forgiveness. I believe, You died for my sins and rose from the dead. I turn from my sins and invite You to come into my heart and life. I want to trust and follow You as my Lord and Savior. If you prayed and believe this with all your heart, then welcome to the family.

Bible

There are so many bibles in the market today. I can suggest the ESV, English Standard Version, or the NIV, New International Version. Other Christians want to read from the King James Version because they think since the KJV was the earliest to release here in the United States of America, it must be the most correct version. But it is not. Time has shown that the KJV is not and full of errors. Other people enjoy the New King James Version. Read a reliable bible that you can understand. More times you read the bible, the more you will understand the bible. Just keep reading.

Dedicated to

Dedicated to my parents for the memories.

Also, to my family for the encouragement and to God for the strength.

May God Bless You

Printed in Great Britain
by Amazon